Evil

Paul Ricoeur

Evil

A Challenge to Philosophy and Theology

Translated by John Bowden

Introduction by Graham Ward

continuum

Continuum
The Tower Building   80 Maiden Lane
11 York Road   Suite 704
London   New York
SE1 7NX   NY 10038

www.continuumbooks.com

Translated by John Bowden from the French *Le mal. Un défi à la philosophie et à la théologie*, third edition, published by Editions Labor et Fides, Geneva.

© 2004 Editions Labor et Fides

First published in English by Continuum, 2007.
Copyright © Continuum, 2007

British Library Cataloguing-in-Publication Data
A catalogue record for this book is available from the British Library.

ISBN 0 8264 9476 5

Typeset by BookEns Ltd, Royston, Herts.
Printed and bound by Ashford Colour Press Ltd, Gosport, Hampshire

Contents

Introduction

Introduction

Paul Ricoeur was 72 when he delivered the lecture that formed the basis for this essay, having been born in France in the year just prior to the outbreak of the First World War. That he grew up and matured as an intellectual in the context of two world wars, each of which impacted deeply upon France, goes some way to explaining why conflict is so predominant a theme in his writings. In the Second World War he was interned in a German prisoner-of-war camp. But by 1985, when he gave this lecture, he was a giant among twentieth-century philosophers, with a reputation established on works that embraced moral philosophy, hermeneutics and phenomenology. Behind him stood books such as *Freedom and Nature: The Voluntary and the Involuntary* (1950), *Fallible Man* (1960), *The Symbolism of Evil* (1960), *Freud and Philosophy* (1965) and *The Rule of Metaphor* (1975). He had just completed for publication in that year the third and final volume of his massive and influential study *Time and Narrative* (1985) and had begun work on what would become *Oneself as Another* (1990). Before he died in 2005 he had also written *Memory, History and Forgetting* (2000) and *The Course of Recognition* (2004). He also wrote over 500 essays.

The titles of Ricoeur's works betray two of his abiding interests: the examination of what it is to be human, which is part of the distinctive move French existential phenomenologists made with respect to the German legacies of Husserl and Heidegger; and the nature of interpretation. The titles also betray some of the influences on his philosophy: the German thinking of Kant, Hegel, Dilthey and Freud and the French thinking of Blondel, Marcel, Bloch and Braudel. Although often perceived religiously in terms of his Protestant upbringing and faith, which finds expression in his interpretative essays on the Bible and his phenomenological analyses of revelation and testimony, in fact his specific examination of philosophical anthropology and its relation to language bring him closer in thought to Augustine. Like Augustine, Ricoeur was drawn to profundity and the inexhaustible nature of interpreting signs and symbols, metaphors and stories; what he once called 'the richness of the real'.[1] Like Augustine also, the

---

[1] 'Philosophy of Will and Action', in Charles E. Regan and David Stewart (eds), *The Philosophy of Paul Ricoeur: An Anthology of his Work*, Boston: Beacon Press, 1978, p. 70.

question of evil was never far from his interrogation of the perplexities of human actions and intentions, time and the written composition of such actions and intentions.

Ricoeur's approach to philosophy – and here most particularly the question of evil – eschews abstractions and reductions in favour of the rich complexities of action and practice, the nuanced densities and varieties of text and the conflict of interpretations. The mysterious and the allusive caught his imagination and triggered the rigorousness of his philosophical investigation. His earlier work, perhaps up to and including *Time and Narrative*, unravels layers of this complexity and conflict and seeks to locate a mediating position. And so it is that commentators upon Ricoeur have emphasized the Hegelian holism of his method. But his later work, *Oneself as Another*, strikes, to my mind, a different note, and it is with respect to that new note that this present essay on evil, and the challenge its subtitle alludes to become significant. (*Défi* is the language of combat, from it we have the English word 'defiance'.) *Time and Narrative* examines a conflict between the aporetics or multiple ambivalences of time and poetics or the means and modes of narrative. Reading and the interpretation of narrative that configures and refigures the experience of time in and through language, mediates between these conflicting positions. Thus the aporetics of experienced time and the poetics of narrative belong each to the other. This is a rapid summary of a very sophisticated piece of textual and philosophical analysis extending over almost 800 pages in the English translation. Justice cannot be done to it. But the summary points to the affirmative humanism that dominates Ricoeur's understanding of what it is to be human. In *Oneself as Another* 'aporia', taken to be an abyss in human understanding, assumes a more profound and not so easily resolved focus. The rupturing diachrony of otherness as it is explored in the philosophy of Levinas opens up an undecidability quite different in tone from the work of mediating between conflicting positions. The other remains, philosophically, utterly equivocal and unknowable: another person, the shadow of past ancestors dwelling in the very constitution of oneself, the living God, the absent God or just an empty place. With the thought of the other, Ricoeur concludes, philosophy comes to an end. It is as if the mystery of human transcendence, which Ricoeur had explored clearly and with acuity, finally engulfs him in this late work. Hegelian mediation

gives ground to Kantian antinomy, and particularly the aporia of radical evil, with which Kant
opened his examination of *Religion within the
Limits of Reason Alone*.

We will return to Ricoeur's interpretation in
Oneself as Another and of Kant's notion of radical
evil in a moment. As mentioned above, this book
was published five years after the essay we have
here, and Ricoeur's exploration of moral evil
began much earlier. His philosophy of the will, as
it developed in his first work, *Freedom and Nature*,
proceeded by raising a Kantian antinomy between
the body and consciousness and demonstrating
the reciprocity between the two positions. The
infinite possibilities of freedom are circumscribed
by the limitations of nature and human experience
is the temporal wing out of these two trajectories.
In the further two volumes of the philosophy of
will, *Fallible Man* and *Symbolism of Evil*, the
governing antinomy of the finite and the infinite
are explored in terms of this experience of being
human, and it is here that Ricoeur opens up the
question of evil.

The exploration of the finite and the infinite
and the mediation between them is part of
Descartes' and Kant's legacy to the early German
Romantics. Descartes' analysis in the fourth of his

Meditations on the innate sense that human beings have of the perfect, which leads them to understand the infinitity of their own imperfections, and Kant's allusion to a radical evil that presents a limit to what is rational, are never far from Ricoeur's own thinking. But Ricoeur's analysis deepens the epistemological interests of Descartes and Kant, drawing something from both the Romantic concern with passion and affectivity, and also the French phenomenological concern with embodiment. The finite and the infinite are not abstractions but human experiences of knowing, acting and feeling, and therefore open to analysis; experiences that betray 'human reality ... [as] not coinciding with itself'.[2] If human beings are 'reconciler[s] of the extreme poles of the real'[3] there is a fragility about this reconciliation or mediation. The fragility arises because the infinite aspires to a totality in which all things are integrated. This aspiration to unity is the same as the idea of happiness. It was Augustine who first suggested that what human beings desire most is happiness: happiness as a primordial affirmation,

---

[2] *Fallible Man*, tr. Charles A. Kelbley, New York: Fordham University Press, 1986, p. 133.
[3] Ibid., p. 141.

what Ricoeur calls 'the Joy of Yes'[4] that being human announces. But this original Joy is troubled by feelings of dependence; the knowledge that the other is never myself; experiences of the precariousness of living; of birth and death. These limitations and imperfections confront the primordial affirmation with the sadness of finitude. Here is the ultimate conflict and paradox which human beings mediate: this none coincidence of infinite Joy and finite sadness. Moral evil issues, for Ricoeur, from this none coincidence; from the fissure of fallibility that this condition opens up.

But fallibility is not yet fault – only the capacity for failing. 'Capacity' is an important term here because it returns us to the heart of the problem Ricoeur is examining: the will to act. Fallibility is associated with a power to act. Human beings have the *power* to fail. In fact, it is when they fail, when they do evil, that the fallibility most reveals itself. The last few pages of *Fallible Man* hover on the edges of this fallibility that is not yet fault, probing the hiatus that separates them. In the

---

[4] Ibid., p. 140. Gisel refers to this primordial affirmation [*l'affirmation originaire*] in his Preface to the essay, but he does not define what Ricoeur means by this notion.

book that follows, *The Symbolism of Evil*, the line is crossed, examining the expressions of failing, the symbolics of evil and the myths of its origin. In these representations, the original affirmation is isolated from the subsequent failure; goodness and the state of innocence are distinguished from the act of erring, of falling away. Such isolation and distinction is only possible, Ricoeur argues, when perceived imaginatively. In the everyday experience of knowing, acting and feeling such distinctions are impossible; this is our existential condition.

To disclose the profound aporia in what it is to be human is, for Ricoeur, as far as philosophy can go. Theology, of course, goes much further. But when Ricoeur enters the theological worldview, as in *The Symbolism of Evil*, he encounters a world of myths and metaphors. The phenomenological challenges of *Fallible Man* now engage the hermeneutical challenges of the theological imagination. What is important to understand as we take up this present essay is that the mystery of evil itself is never confronted directly in this early analysis. It lies between the philosophy of fallibility and the theological expressions of fault, in the hiatus between the last two volumes of his philosophy of the will. Evil is the excess, the disproportion, within being human *that* being human cannot fathom. But we can observe here already that it places a stumbling-block that no philosophy of mediation (such as Hegel's, for example) can negotiate. As such, it points to the limits of Ricoeur's own philosophical mediation of conflict. Just when it seems that all things can be brought together in a grand synthesis, each belonging reciprocally to the other, the question of evil arises like a dark apocalyptic angel disturbing the waters. The angel commands that Ricoeur think again, which perhaps accounts for the exploratory and essayistic character of his writing.

It is therefore perhaps not so surprising to discover that Ricoeur, having completed his trilogy, *Time and Narrative* (1985), returns in this essay to the question of evil. The enormous intellectual venture into poetics, rhetoric and hermeneutics which began in *The Symbolism of Evil* and continued in *The Rule of Metaphor* comes to its conclusion. In that third volume, Ricoeur, the advocate of a Hegelian synthesis in which the aporetics of time are enfolded into the poetics' narrative and the poetics of narrative explicate the aporetics of time, posits throughout the move-ment of historical consciousness towards the unity of history. Mediation is again at the forefront of his philosophical task, when the dark angel returns. In *Oneself as Another* it is to Kant's reflection on radical evil that Ricoeur turns. He carefully dissects Kant's argument, in which the human propensity [*Hang*] for good, out of which universalizable maxims emerge, is crossed by an equally natural predisposition to self-love, out of which bad maxims emerge. His reading of Kant is more nuanced here than in this essay, where Kant's anthropology is captured too neatly between the human propensity for evil and the human predisposition towards the good. But the conclusion is the same: the origin of evil is understood to reside in the nature of human freedom; the exercise of freedom reveals evil to us, just as evil itself reveals the nature of freedom. Drawn to Kant's use of 'radical', that which goes to the very roots of the human condition, Ricoeur will speak of evil as an aporia that cannot be mediated; it is inscrutable, its origins enigmatic.[5] In this essay he will speak of 'the demonic depth of human freedom' (p. 53). In *Oneself as Another* he recognizes the dualism this encourages in Kant:

---

[5] *Oneself as Another*, tr. Kathleen Blamey, Chicago: University of Chicago Press, 1992, pp. 215–18.

'We, in fact, see that Kant is careful to preserve something of the Augustinian tradition [of original sin] – by making the penchant for evil a quasi nature, to the point of declaring the penchant for evil to be *innate* – all the while assuming a deliberately Pelagian stance.'[6] The use of 'quasi' is interesting. For Kant, evil is not a 'quasi nature' but 'a natural propensity'.[7] But by using 'quasi' Ricoeur softens the dualism, which is not only Kant's but also his as a legatee of Kant's thinking in favour of the predisposition to the good. It is a tiny sleight of hand that demonstrates Ricoeur's own humanist inclinations; a humanism that because of the inscrutability of evil cannot be founded upon philosophical grounds. Again, the question of evil draws philosophy towards its own limit.

In the context, then, of Ricoeur's philosophical and hermeneutical engagements with evil, what is significant about this essay is its attention to theology, a discourse which to Ricoeur, it seems, issues from philosophy's own fallibilities. If

---

[6] Ibid., p. 217.
[7] *Religion within the Limits of Reason Alone*, tr. Theodore M. Greene and Hoyt H. Hudson, New York: Harper & Row, 1960, p. 32.

philosophical discourse shows human beings coming to a knowledge of themselves and their openness to a transcending horizon, then theological discourse shows human beings coming to a knowledge about their relation to God, a knowledge rooted in God's own self-revelation. The first discourse is analytical and the second is confessional, because in part it comes from elsewhere (and that is why it is only on the basis of belief and confession, that it can take its place among the sciences). If we examine what is distinctive about Ricoeur's approach to theology in this essay, two significant points emerge. The first is his opening examination of the 'experience of evil'. Recall that earlier approaches to evil took place in terms of either a philosophy of will or the interpretation of signs (myths, symbols, metaphors); they were governed by epistemological and hermeneutical questions. Now we have a new account: of evil suffered, not just the analysis of the aporia in which evil takes place or finds representation. In fact myth is explicitly understood as not being capable of delivering an answer to the question of evil. There is an appreciation of the genre of lament, simple complaint.

The cry of pain sharpens the philosophical questioning, developing a genre of wisdom

writing and a moral vision of the world that
eventually produces theodicies. But, before this
morphing of wisdom into theodicy, Ricoeur
indicates another line of thinking that is again a
significant departure in his own work: the need to
examine the ontological question of evil as it arises
for theology itself. To embark on this approach is
to return to a much older tradition that Ricoeur
relates to Augustine. Behind the onto-theology of
Leibniz, and theodicy more generally (which
conflated ontology with epistemology, structures
of being with structures of knowing), lay the
tradition of the early Greek and Latin Fathers. In
this historical perspective – which is still very
Hegelian – in which myth gives way to rational
theology, Ricoeur situates Augustine's twin concerns with ontology and theology as a stage on the
way to the development of theodicy. This a
questionable development, but all would agree
that 'Theodicy in the strict sense is the flagship of
onto-theology' (p. 49). For the onto-theological
trajectory of thinking, evil was ultimately an
epistemological issue in which knowledge could
be reduced to a series of propositions that
accorded with the two basic rules of logic: they
were non-contradictory and they cohered, that is
they formed part of a rational system. Ricoeur

demonstrates that the irrational leaves such an onto-theological approach itself begging. The older trajectory of thinking only spoke of evil in terms of a privation of being. As such, evil lay outside any onto-theological possibility because in and of itself it had no substance. That was not to say that evil did not occur; Augustine and Ricoeur do not make such a claim. In Augustine's understanding, evil was non-being, and only as such could it be seen as not in dualistic opposition to the good. Its occurrence then was contrary to and working against the orders of existence. The point here, philosophically and theologically, is: what kind of existence does evil actually have?

We have to be very clear about what it means for Ricoeur to raise such a question – the explorer looking for the mediation of conflict, the philosopher who looked always to an original affirmation about human beings and a final horizon of history in which an ultimate synthesis will be demonstrated. For the move he makes in the latter part of his essay is novel: the radical shift away from a Hegelian to a Barthian understanding of dialectic. Barth scholarship has begun to reject the idea that Barth 'replied to Hegel' to use Ricoeur's language (p. 59) by employing a Kierkegaardian appreciation of dialectic. Nevertheless, Ricoeur's point would stand: Barth's thinking cuts right across the project of onto-theology with its intimation of a systematic totalization. Although Ricoeur does not end his argument with Barth, pointing to how his broken dialectic culminates in paradox bordering on contradiction, he draws his conclusion on the basis of Barth's polemical stance against onto-theology that 'the aporia in which thought about evil finds itself' (p. 64) has to be recognized. This is, as we saw above, the position he takes at the end of *Oneself as Another.*

Aporia, the hiatus in knowledge, the abyss in human understanding, is the last word in the philosophical argument of this essay, the final part of which returns us to wisdom and the work of mourning. These are responses, not answers, to evil that leave the primordial affirmation of being human somewhat muted. But this does not obliterate Ricoeur's perennial optimism, the ultimate note of the essay is utopic: the notion of a time when 'violence has been suppressed' and 'the enigma of true suffering, of irreducible suffering, will be laid bare' (p. 72). Ricoeur has always viewed utopic thinking as important; it offers a critical and imaginative alternative to the status quo. But the dark angel has stirred the waters and the rippling will not easily subside; it will still be there five years later with his next volume, and even in this essay, when all violence has been expunged, the irreducibility of suffering remains.

Graham Ward
University of Manchester

Preface

The text set out here is that of a lecture which Paul Ricoeur gave at the Faculty of Theology of Lausanne University in 1985. It is devoted to a question which dogged Paul Ricoeur throughout his reflection and his philosophical works: the reality of evil as questioning a certain way of thinking (namely, what he calls theodicy and onto-theology). Over and above that, there is the obligation to take up again the theme of *primordial affirmation*, both of the self's quest for individual and collective existence and of God, that crosses through the signs which human beings inscribe on the heart of creation.[1]

Paul Ricoeur has Protestant roots. They can be emphasized without any desire to claim him for Protestantism or to defend him. That is first of all because Paul Ricoeur has never hidden this origin nor the solidarity that it entails for him; he has simply wanted to indicate clearly and legitimately who he was: he wanted to be a philosopher and not a theologian. Secondly, to draw attention to his Protestant roots here is not meant to imply any superiority, but to place him at a point in history,

---

[1] Ricoeur has written numerous works; see here especially his 'intellectual autobiography', *Réflexion faite*, Paris: Éditions du Seuil, 1995.

with its strong points but also with the awareness that all strong points can have their specific opposites.[2] Paul Ricoeur seems to me to be typically Protestant precisely in his way of putting the question of evil in a place which, for human beings, is a place of origin. This decision makes it necessary – here again in a typically Protestant fashion – from the start to part company with any unifying perspective which speaks too quickly – without any break in its origin and at a directly rational level – of Christian cosmology (with its possible derivations, such as Christian anthropology, Christian ethics and politics).[3]

The titles of several of Paul Ricoeur's works already indicate that he has always grappled with the question of evil. We should note especially *Finitude and Guilt* (in two parts: *Fallible Man* and

---

[2] For the kind of Protestantism envisaged here see the relevant articles in Pierre Gisel (ed.), *Encyclopédie du protestantisme*, Paris: Editions du Cerf and Geneva: Labor et Fides, 1995.

[3] The originally Protestant 'gesture' substitutes for a Christian cosmology (or a Christian anthropology, politics or ethics) a theological position on the question of the world (or a theological position on the question of human beings, politics, ethical questions and so on).

The Symbolism of Evil),[4] the article on 'Original Sin' (1960) reproduced in *The Conflict of Interpretations*,[5] or another study, picking up 'Religion, Atheism, and Faith',[6] namely 'Guilt, Ethics and Religion'.[7] In this context, it should again be emphasized that Paul Ricoeur constantly looks towards Kant, who is at the same time a philosopher of limits, of 'radical evil', and of a way of inaugurating a philosophy of culture, religion or art which is a deliberately practical philosophy, a philosophy with a task under the sign of a hope that is well understood.

Over and above these references, I think that the very career of Paul Ricoeur is typical here. I shall describe it briefly. His major work of the 1950s and 1960s is *Philosophy of the Will*, written in the key of a phenomenology inherited from

---

[4] Paul Ricoeur, *Fallible Man*, New York: Fordham University Press, 1986; *The Symbolism of Evil*, Boston: Beacon Press, 1969.

[5] Paul Ricoeur, *The Conflict of Interpretations*, Evanston, IL: Northwestern University Press, 1974.

[6] Ibid., pp. 440–67.

[7] Ibid., pp. 425–39. See also the Prefaces to Olivier Reboul, *Kant et le problème du mal*, Montreal: Presses de l'Université de Montréal, 1971, or Jean Nabert, *Le désir de Dieu*, Paris: Aubier, 1966.

Husserl. However, his choice to devote himself to an analysis of the will is probably not an innocent one (at all events it leads him to take the dimensions of the body more deliberately into account). Nor is it the emphasis on the involuntary that puts a strain on the voluntary – and also, in some respects, provokes it.[8] Above all, emphasis must be laid on the move made at the beginning of *Symbolism of Evil*. Here we have an interruption of pure, neutral description; we note – we have to note – the way in which the effective fault is disregarded. Now this shift is not a movement as such. No description could move from innocence to the fault.[9] So another method – another posture in philosophizing – will be required: a hermeneutic, an interpretation of signs (whether religious or mythological) which expresses both the acknowledgement of the fault and the hope that it will be overtaken in action. It is the symbol which here 'makes one think'.[10] This way cannot be ignored. Why? Because evil is bound up with the enigma of

---

[8] *Paul Ricoeur, Philosophie de la volonté*, Paris: Aubier, 1950; the title of the first volume is *Le volontaire et l'involontaire*.

[9] Cf. *Fallible Man* (n. 4), p. xlii.

[10] *The Symbolism of Evil* (n. 4), p. 324.

a sudden appearance that cannot be included among the simple things of the world which spread themselves in time and space.

This is the movement that Paul Ricoeur takes up when he breaks with 'theodicy' and 'onto-theology'. He follows the same course over 'original sin' in his exemplary study of St Augustine. For Ricoeur, thought – whether theological or philosophical – must always conquer itself afresh in the face of its internal temptations. It can do so by looking from the perspective of the non-philosophical sources which precede it, accompany it and overhang it: the religious expressions *par excellence* and, over and beyond that, the realities that they crystallize – those of evil, of existence itself and of God. As for existence, the present text is rightly instructive in emphasizing, perhaps more than Ricoeur had previously done, the realities of complaint, protest – one might say obstinate individuality.[11] Job, who is invoked later, is the exemplary figure.

Over and above these observations, which set out only to give a context to the present text, can

---

[11] Cf. also, on this topic, Paul Ricoeur, 'Le récit interprétatif', *Recherches de science religieuse*, 1985/1, pp. 18ff.

we take up more systematically what is involved in thinking and existing? Perhaps, but only as an introduction to and summary of the texts of Paul Ricoeur himself, with all due reservations.

Here are a few points to provide a stimulus to reading them.

The first point to note is that evil is not a thing, an element of the world, a substance in any natural sense.[12] The Church Fathers emphasized this, as did the medieval doctors, setting themselves against all gnosticism (any thought of evil in the principal form of knowledge). If evil were 'world' (and the same goes for God), myth would be knowledge. Now philosophy is sometimes an offshoot of a mythical knowledge, which is why it has to start with a critique of illusion (its own and that of every human being),[13] a critique of idols (its own), a critique of its forms of 'rational theology'. By contrast, evil necessarily comes under the problem of freedom. That is why one can be responsible for it, take it upon oneself,

---

[12] Cf. especially *The Conflict of Interpretations* (n. 5), pp. 270f.

[13] Cf. in Kant, the critique of the transcendental illusion, put to death by speculative theology, which alone can open up the field of practical reason and the interpretation of human texts and works.

confess it and fight it. That is to say that evil is on the side neither of sensibility nor of the body (as such, these are innocent),[14] nor is it on the side of reason (human beings would be deliberately and utterly diabolical). Evil is inscribed on the heart of the human subject (the subject of a law or a moral subject), on the heart of the extremely complex and deliberately historical reality which makes up the human subject.

Evil falls under a problem of freedom, or morality. So it is not a matter of being imprisoned in being or cosmic fatalism. Is the solution then 'Pelagian', putting all the weight on the free decision of human beings, capable of inventing good *or* evil? No, despite his equivocations or the weight of his formulations, St Augustine and the concept of 'original sin' are true, theologically and humanly. The human will never begins by being neutral, without a history, without habits, without a nature that has been acquired and constructed, in fact and by origin.[15] Why? That is the point at which everything holds together or dissolves: because human beings are subjects only when they are called, when they are responsible. Kant

---

[14] Preface to Reboul, *Kant et le problème du mal* (n. 7), p. x.
[15] Cf. *The Conflict of Interpretations* (n. 5), p. 277.

says that we face a law which makes us think (and therefore in a sense be) other than pure nature. What we are marks and makes the difference. We break away; we are singular. Now to be called is to be 'elected': it is to relate to God. And because what we have here is both concrete, particular, contingent history and at the same time history without paradox, original, as a constitutive place or a place of coming forth, only myth and the religious allow us to give it expression. For Paul Ricoeur and the tradition which he takes up, to meditate on evil is to express a natural fault at the heart of all that is imprisoned in being, and radically to lean on this break in order to be, to be human. In this sense evil (like God) does not relate to a single unfolding of time; it is bound up with what 'happened once for all',[16] before which my effective freedom is summed up, called and provoked to exist.

Paul Ricoeur has his place in the heritage of a reflective philosophy, a philosophy for which the original affirmation belongs in the sphere of interiority, taking up the self again. But the fact of evil bends this philosophy. It cuts it off from a

---

[16] Cf. the Preface to Reboul, *Kant et le problème du mal* (n. 7), p. x.

temptation to state the human subject as an 'auto-position'. It decentres this subject, sets it in an order of doing and there summons it to a deepening which, without abandoning contingency in any way, issues in a meditation on the absolute (that which is not tied).

The divine does not have any 'substrate' of its own in the order of the world because nothing in the world is or can be divine as such (here we are talking strictly about the divine, as we shall shortly be talking about evil). It is transcendence, and as such it makes light of the birth of the human subject and its access to existence, when this human subject comes up against a break which is both original and within time; can confess its past as something that has taken place and not as simple destiny; can speak of its present as its own birth and can open itself to welcome what is to come. It must be emphasized that the fact of existence is at issue here, as a gift: for human beings, existence is received, and that is why they do not belong to themselves.

Paul Ricoeur is a philosopher in the full sense of the word, not simply a methodologist in the interpretative sciences or a psycho-sociologist of historical narratives. So for him the internal differences and breaks within history and the world are not to be surmounted – reduced? – by a simple use of appropriate methods. That would be a technical or functionalist approach, which conceals what is at stake. The differences and the ruptures that weave our existences together are assumed and taken charge of, to be referred to as an essential, constitutive break, that about which everything turns, that which allows – which institutes – the particularities, the densities of each present, the singularity of persons. To make an appeal from this to transcendence[17] takes priority: it cannot be reduced to the simple future inscribed in passing time. It is this that makes possible memory – anamnesis or *making* remembrance – of the past, of the real, of the life of human beings in the body and of what they do (poietics) or what happens to them (teleology).

Pierre Gisel

---

[17] It is from the beginning of *Le volontaire et l'involontaire* (n. 8) that the destiny of the questions of evil (or, more precisely, the fault) and transcendence are linked (pp. 7, 31ff.); from that point it is also said that transcendence conceals 'the radical origin of subjectivity' (p. 7).

Evil: A Challenge to
Philosophy and Theology

Sometimes complaining bitterly, the greatest thinkers in both philosophy and theology agree that both these disciplines encounter evil as an unparalleled challenge. What is important is not this admission, but the way in which the challenge, indeed the setback, is received: is it an invitation to think less or a provocation to think more, indeed to think differently?

What the problem puts in question is a way of thinking which is subject to the demands of logical consistency; that is to say, thinking that is at once not a contradiction and yet concerned with systematic totality. This is the dominant way of thinking in attempts at theodicy in the technical sense of the word. However different these attempts may be in the answers that they give, they define the problem in similar terms. How is it possible to affirm at the same time, without contradiction, the following three propositions: God is all-powerful, God is absolutely good, yet evil exists? In that case theodicy seems to be a struggle for coherence, responding to the objection that only two of these propositions are compatible, never all three together. What is presupposed in this way of posing the problem is not itself put in question, namely the propositional form in which the terms of the problem are expressed and the rule of consistency which it is thought that the solution must satisfy.

No account is taken of the fact that these propositions express an 'onto-theological' state of thought which it has taken an advanced stage of speculation to achieve. This thought depends on a fusion between the confessional language of religion and a discourse on the radical origin of all things dating from the period of pre-Kantian metaphysics. Leibniz's theodicy demonstrates this to perfection. Nor is any account taken of the fact that the task of thinking – of thinking of God and thinking of evil before God – cannot be exhausted by our reasoning, which is modelled on non-contradiction, and our proneness to systematic totalization.

To demonstrate the limited and relative character of the position of the problem within the framework of the argument about theodicy, it is important, first, to assess the magnitude and complexity of the problem with the resources of a phenomenology of the experience of evil. Then a distinction must be made between the levels of discourse covered by speculation on the origin and reason for evil. Finally, the work of thinking provoked by the enigma must be related to answers relating to action and feeling.

I. The experience of evil: between reprimand and lamentation

The whole enigma of evil is that, at least in the tradition of the Judaeo-Christian West, as a first approximation we subsume quite disparate phenomena, such as sin, suffering and death, under the same term. It can even be said that it is to the degree that suffering is constantly taken as a term of reference that the question of evil differs from that of sin and guilt. So before saying what points in the direction of a profound common enigma in the phenomenon of evil perpetrated and evil suffered, it is necessary to emphasize that in principle there is a disparity between them.

Strictly speaking, moral evil – sin in religious language – denotes that which makes human action an object of imputation, accusation and reprimand. Imputation consists in attributing an action capable of moral assessment to a responsible subject. Accusation characterizes the action itself as a violation of the ethical code dominant in the community in question. Reprimand denotes a condemnation by virtue of which the author of the action is declared guilty and deserving of punishment. It is here that moral evil interferes with suffering, to the degree that the punishment is a suffering that is inflicted.

Also strictly speaking, suffering differs from sin in that it has contrary features. Suffering emphasizes that the imputation which centres moral evil on a responsible agent is essentially something that is undergone: we do not make it happen, but it affects us. Hence the surprising variety of its causes: the adversity of physical nature, sicknesses and weaknesses of the body and the mind, affliction brought on by the death of those dear to us, the terrifying prospect of our own mortality, the feeling of personal worthlessness, and so on. In contrast to accusation, which denounces a moral deviation, suffering is characterized as the sheer opposite to pleasure: as non-pleasure; that is, as a diminution of our physical, psychological and spiritual integrity. Finally and above all, suffering sets lamentation against reprimand, for if misdeeds make people guilty, suffering makes them victims. That is what lamentation proclaims.

That being the case, what is it that invites philosophy and theology to think of evil as the common root of sin and suffering, despite this indisputable polarity? First of all, the extraordinary way in which these two phenomena are entangled. On the one hand, punishment is a physical and moral suffering over and above moral evil, whether this is corporal punishment, deprivation of freedom, shame or remorse. That is why guilt is itself called a punishment, a term which straddles the break between evil committed and evil undergone. On the other hand, a principal cause of suffering is the violence inflicted by one person on another: doing evil is in fact always doing wrong to another, making another suffer, whether directly or indirectly. In its relational – dialogical – structure, evil committed by one is replicated in the evil undergone by another; it is at this major interface that the cry of lament is most bitter, when one person feels himself the victim of another's wickedness. Both the Psalms of David and Marx's analysis of the alienation arising from the reduction of human beings to commodities bear witness to this.

We are brought one degree further in the direction of a unique mystery of iniquity by the feeling that sin, suffering and death express the profound unity of the human condition in a multiple way. Certainly, here we reach the point where a hermeneutic of symbols and myths takes over from the phenomenology of evil; these symbols and myths offer the first linguistic mediation for what is a confused and speechless experience. Two indicators relating to the experience of evil point in the direction of this profound unity. First, from the side of moral evil, the incrimination of a responsible agent isolates the clearest zone of the experience of guilt from a shadowy background. In depth, this harbours the feeling of having been seduced by superior forces which myth has no trouble in demonizing. In so doing, myth is only expressing the sense of belonging to a history of evil, which is always already there for everyone. The most visible effect of this strange experience of passivity at the very heart of doing evil is that human beings feel themselves victims while at the same time being guilty. We can see the same disruption of the borderline between guilty and victim if we start from the other pole. Since suffering is a punishment thought to be deserved, who knows whether, in one way or another, all sin is not the punishment of a personal or collective fault, known or unknown? This question, which even in our secularized societies verifies the experience of mourning (which I shall discuss at the end of this book), is reinforced by the parallel demonization that makes suffering and sin the expression of the same baneful powers. That is the shadowy basis which makes evil a unique enigma. It is never completely demythologized.

II. The levels of discourse in speculation about evil

We cannot turn to theodicies in the strict sense of the term, with their concern for an absence of contradiction and systematic totalization, without covering several levels of discourse from which a growing rationality emerges.

1. The level of myth

Myth is certainly the first major transition, in several respects.

First, the ambivalence of the sacred as *tremendum fascinosum*, according to Rudolf Otto, confers on myth the power of assuming both the shadow side and the light side of the human condition. Myth, then, incorporates the fragmentary experience of evil in the grand narratives of the beginning with a cosmic scope, in which anthropogenesis becomes part of cosmogenesis. The whole of Mircea Eliade's work bears witness to this. In saying that the world had a beginning, myth relates how the human condition was brought about in its universally wretched form. According to Clifford Geertz, the great religions have kept the major ideological function of this quest for global intelligibility, namely to integrate ethos and cosmos in an all-encompassing vision. That is why, in later stages, the problem of evil would become the major crisis for religion.

However, the corollary and corrective of the function of the order of myth, which according to Georges Dumézil is bound up with its cosmic scope, is the profusion of its explanatory schemes. As the literatures of the ancient East, India and the Far East attest, the domain of myth proves to be a vast experimental workshop, indeed a game, with the most varied and fantastic hypotheses. There is no conceivable solution relating to the entire order of things, and thus the enigma of evil, that has not been tried in this immense laboratory. The comparative history of religions and cultural anthropology put in place typologies which distribute mythical explanations between monism, dualism, mixed solutions and so on, in order to master this infinite variety. The abstract character of these taxonomies, which derive from an inevitable methodological artifice, must not mask the ambiguities and paradoxes, often shrewdly calculated, that are cultivated by most myths at the precise moment of explaining the origin of evil. This is witnessed to by the biblical narrative of the fall, which is open to many other interpretations than the one which has been predominant in the Christian West, mainly following St Augustine. These abstract classifications must not mask the great oscillations within the mythical realm itself, between representations bordering down below on legendary narrative and folklore and up above on metaphysical speculation, of the kind that we can see in the great treatises of Hindu thought. Nevertheless, it is through its aspect as folklore that myth contemplates the demonic side of the experience of evil, articulating it in a language. Conversely, it is through its speculative aspect that it prepares the way for rational theodicies, putting the emphasis on the problems of the beginning. For philosophies and theologies the question raised is: 'Where does evil come from?'

2. The stage of wisdom

Could myth entirely meet the expectations of human beings in their actions and sufferings? Partially, to the degree that it encountered an *interrogation* contained in the lamentation itself: 'How long?', 'Why?' To this, myth brought only the consolation of order, putting the complaint of the one who made it in the framework of an immense universe. But myth gave no answer to an important part of the question: not just 'Why?', but 'Why me?' Here the lamentation becomes a complaint: it asks the deity to give an account. For example, in the biblical sphere, an important implication of the covenant is that it verges on the dimension of role-sharing, of putting on trial. Now, if the Lord is putting his people on trial, his people are also putting their God on trial.

Suddenly, myth has to change key: it has not only to relate the origins of the world in order to explain how the human condition in general came to be what it is, but also to engage in argument, in order to explain why it is as it is for everyone. This is the stage of wisdom. The first and most tenacious of the explanations offered by wisdom is that of retribution: all suffering is deserved because it is punishment for an individual or collective sin, known or unknown. This explanation at least has the advantage of taking suffering seriously as such, as a pole distinct from moral evil. But at the same time it tries to abolish this difference, making the whole order of things a moral order. In this sense, the theory of retribution is the first of the moral visions of the world, to take up an expression that Hegel would apply to Kant. Now because wisdom argues, it had to transform itself into a vast contest with itself, indeed a dramatic debate of wise men within themselves. For retribution could not be a satisfactory answer once a certain legal order began to exist, which distinguished the good from the evil and set out to measure the penalty by the degree of each person's guilt. In the face of even a rudimentary sense of justice, the present distribution of evils can only appear arbitrary, indiscriminate, disproportionate. Why does one person rather than another die of cancer? Why do children die? Why is there so much suffering, in excess of the ordinary capacity of simple mortals to endure?

The book of Job occupies its place in world literature primarily because it takes responsibility for the lamentation which has become a complaint, and for the complaint elevated to the status of a challenge. Taking as the hypothesis of the fable the condition of a righteous sufferer, a just man without faults who is subjected to the worst possible trials, it elevates the internal debate within wisdom to the level of a powerfully argued dialogue between Job and his friends, spurred on by the discord between moral evil and evil as suffering. But the book of Job perhaps moves us even more by the enigmatic and possibly deliberately ambiguous character of its conclusion. The final theophany does not give any direct reply to

Job's personal suffering; the speculation remains open in several directions: the vision of a creator with unfathomable designs, of an architect whose measurements are incompatible with human fortunes, can suggest that the consolation is differentiated eschatologically, that the complaint is out of place and inopportune, in respect of a God who is master of good and evil (according to the saying in Isaiah 45.7, 'I form light and I create darkness, I make weal and create woe'), or that the complaint itself must undergo one of the purifying trials which I shall be mentioning in the third part. Aren't Job's last words, 'Therefore I despise myself, and repent in dust and ashes'? What is there to repent of but the complaint itself? And isn't it by virtue of this repentance that Job can love God gratuitously, contrary to Satan's wager at the beginning of the story in which the debate is set?

I shall be returning to these questions in the third part; for the moment I shall limit myself to following the thread of the speculation opened up by wisdom.

3. The stage of gnosticism and anti-gnostic gnosis

Thought would not have moved from wisdom to theodicy had not gnosticism elevated speculation to the status of a fight between giants in which the forces of good are engaged in merciless combat with the armies of evil, aimed at the deliverance of all the particles of light held captive in the darkness of matter. This is the Augustinian retort to this tragic vision, in which all the figures of evil are assumed into a principle of evil, and it has formed one of the foundations of Western thought. I shall not discuss sin and guilt thematically here, but limit myself to aspects of Augustine's teaching that relate to the place of suffering in a global interpretation of evil. In fact it is to gnosticism that Western thought is indebted for having raised the problem of evil as a problematical totality: *unde malum?* (where does evil come from?).

Augustine could oppose the tragic view of gnosticism (which is usually classified among the dualistic solutions, without taking account of the specific epistemological level of this very special dualism), first because he was able to borrow from philosophy, specifically from Neoplatonism, a conceptual apparatus capable of wrecking the conceptual aspect of a rationalized myth. Augustine remembers from the philosophers that evil cannot be regarded as a *substance*, because to think 'being' is to think 'intelligible', to think 'one', to think 'well'. So it is philosophical thought that excludes any fantasy of a substantive evil. In return, a new idea of nothingness appears, that of *ex nihilo*, contained in the idea of a creation that is total and without remainder. At the same time, another negative concept develops, associated with the previous one, namely that of an ontic distance between the creator and the creature which makes it possible to speak of the deficiency of the created as such: by virtue of this deficiency it becomes comprehensible that creatures endowed with free choice can 'decline' far from God and 'incline' towards that which has less being, towards nothingness.

This first feature of Augustine's teaching deserves to be recognized for what it is, namely the conjunction of ontology and theology in a new type of discourse, onto-theology.

The most important corollary of this negation of the substantiality of evil is that the admission of evil is the basis of an exclusively moral vision of evil. If the question *unde malum*? loses all its ontological significance, the question which replaces it, *unde malum faciamus*? ('how does it come about that we do evil'), tips the whole problem of evil over into the sphere of action, of the will, of free will. Sin introduces a nothingness of a distinct kind, a *nihil privativum*, for which the fall is entirely responsible, whether this is the fall of man or of more elevated creatures such as angels. There is no reason to seek a cause for this nothingness beyond some evil will. The *Contra Fortunatum* draws the conclusion from this moral vision of evil that is most important for us here, namely that all evil is either *peccatum* (sin) or *poena* (punishment); a purely moral vision of evil entails in its turn a penal view of history: no soul has been unjustly precipitated into misfortune.

An enormous price has to be paid for the coherence of the doctrine; and its magnitude inevitably emerges on the occasion of the anti-Pelagian dispute, separated by several decades from the anti-Manichaean dispute. To make credible the idea that all suffering, unjustly distributed or excessive though it may be, is a retribution for sin, sin has to be given a supra-individual dimension, one that is historical, even generic; that is what the doctrine of 'original sin' or 'natural sin' is responding to. I shall not retrace the stages by which it was constructed (the literal interpretation of Genesis 3, handed on through Paul's emphasis in Romans 5.12–19, the justification of infant baptism and so on). I shall merely emphasize the epistemological status or the level of discourse of the dogmatic proposition on original sin. Essentially, this proposition notes a fundamental aspect of the experience of evil, namely the experience of human impotence, both individual and communal, in the face of the demonic power of an evil which is already there before any evil intention that can be attributed to some deliberate intent. But this enigma of the power of evil which is already there is placed in the false clarity of an explanation that appears rational: by combining in the concept of natural sin two heterogeneous notions, that of a biological transmission through procreation and that of an individual imputation of guilt, the notion of original sin appears as a false concept which can be assigned to an anti-gnostic gnosticism. The content of gnosticism is denied, but the form of the discourse of gnosticism, namely that of a rationalized myth, is reconstituted.

That is why Augustine would seem more profound than Pelagius, because he has seen that the nothingness of privation is at the same time a power superior to any individual will and any singular volition. By contrast, Pelagius would appear more truthful, because he leaves every being free in the face of its sole responsibility, as Jeremiah and Ezekiel had done previously by denying that children were paying for the misdeeds of their fathers.

More seriously, Augustine and Pelagius, by offering two opposite versions of a strictly moral vision of evil, leave unanswered the protest against unjust suffering, the former by condemning it to silence in the name of a mass accusation of the human race, the latter by ignoring it in the name of a highly ethical concern for responsibility.

4. *The stage of theodicy*

We have the right to speak of theodicy only when (a) the statement of the problem of evil is based on propositions aimed at univocity; that is the case with the three assertions which are generally considered: God is all-powerful; his goodness is infinite; evil exists; (b) the aim of the argument is clearly apologetic: God is not responsible for evil; (c) the means employed are thought to satisfy the logic of non-contradiction and systematic totality. Now, these conditions have been fulfilled only in the framework of onto-theology, joining terms borrowed from religious discourse, essentially God, and terms relating to metaphysics (for example, Platonic or Cartesian metaphysics), like being, nothingness, first cause, finality, infinite, finite and so on. Theodicy in the strict sense is the flagship of onto-theology.

In this respect, Leibniz's *Theodicy* remains the model of the genre. On the one hand, all the forms of evil, and not only moral evil (as in the Augustinian tradition), but also suffering and death, are taken into consideration and put under the heading of *metaphysical evil*, which is the inescapable flaw in all created beings, if it is true that God would not know how to create another God. On the other hand, classical logic is enriched with the addition of the principle of sufficient reason to the principle of non-contradiction. This sufficient reason states itself as the principle of the better, once one conceives creation as having emerged from a competition in the divine understanding between a multiplicity of models of the world, one of which comprises the maximum of perfections with the minimum of flaws. The notion of the best of all possible worlds, so mocked by Voltaire in *Candide* after the disaster of the Lisbon earthquake, is not understood as long as one does not see in it the rational nerve, namely the calculation of the maximum and the minimum of which our model of the world is the result. It is in this way that the principle of sufficient reason can fill the abyss between the logically possible, i.e. the not-impossible, and the contingent, i.e. that which could be otherwise.

The failure of the *Theodicy*, even within the space of thought marked out by onto-theology, arises from the fact that a finite understanding cannot attain the facts of this grandiose calculation; it can only collect the sparse signs of excess of perfections by comparison with imperfections in the balance of good and evil. In that case a robust human optimism is needed to assert that the balance is overall positive. And as we always have only the crumbs of the principle of the better, we have to content ourselves with its aesthetic corollary, by virtue of which the contrast between the negative and the positive competes with the harmony of the whole. It is precisely this claim to be establishing a positive assessment of the balance of goods and evils on a quasi-aesthetic basis which fails once one is confronted with evils or pains, the excess of which would not seem capable of being compensated by any perfection. Once again it is the lamentation, the complaint of the righteous sufferer, which wrecks the notion of a compensation of evil with good, as it once wrecked the idea of retribution.

The rudest shock to the very basis of onto-theological discourse on which theodicy was built from Augustine to Leibniz, even if it was not fatal, was delivered by Kant. The implacable dismantling of rational theology brought about by the dialectical part of the *Critique of Pure Reason* is well known. Deprived of its ontological support, theodicy falls under the rubric of the 'transcendental illusion'. That is not to say that the problem of evil disappears from the philosophical scene – on the contrary. But it relates only to the practical sphere, as that which must not be and that which action has to fight against. Thus thought once again finds itself in a situation comparable to that to which Augustine had brought it: we cannot ask where evil comes from, but we can ask how it is that we do evil. As in the time of Augustine, the problem of suffering is sacrificed to the problem of moral evil. However, there are two differences.

On the one hand, suffering ceases to be bound up with the sphere of morality on the grounds of punishment. It relates all the more to the teleological judgement of the *Critique of Judgement* which, moreover, authorizes a relatively optimistic assessment of the dispositions with which human beings are endowed by nature, such as the disposition to sociability and personality, dispositions that human beings are called on to cultivate. It is in relation to this moral task that suffering is obliquely taken care of, certainly at the individual level but above all at the level that Kant calls cosmopolitan. The origin of evil and suffering has lost all philosophical relevance.

On the other hand, the problem of radical evil, to which *Religion within the Limits of Reason Alone* opens up, clearly breaks with that of original sin, despite some similarities. Quite apart from the fact that no recourse to juridical and biological schemes confers a fallacious intelligibility on radical evil (in this sense Kant would be more Pelagian than Augustinian), the principle of evil is not in any way an origin in the temporal sense of the term; it is only the supreme maximum which serves as a last subjective foundation for all the evil maxims of our free will. This supreme maximum is the basis for the propensity (*Hang*) towards evil throughout the human race (in this sense Kant is put alongside Augustine) as opposed to the predisposition (*Anlage*) to good which constitutes good will. But the reason for this radical evil is 'inscrutable' (*unerforschbar*): 'we have no comprehensible reason for knowing whence moral evil could first of all have come to us'. Like Karl Jaspers, I admire this last admission: like Augustine and perhaps like mythical thought, it perceives the demonic depth of human freedom, but with the sobriety of a thought which is always careful not to transgress the limits of knowledge and to preserve the distance between thinking and knowing by object.

However, speculative thought does not give up in the face of the problem of evil. Kant did not put an end to rational theology: he forced it to use other resources implicated in this manner of thinking – this *Denken* – that the limitation of knowledge by object put in reserve. The extraordinary flourishing of systems at the time of German idealism bears witness to this: Fichte, Schelling, Hegel, not to mention other giants such as Hamann, Jacobi and Novalis.

The example of Hegel is particularly striking from our point of view here of the levels of discourse, by virtue of the role played by the mode of dialectical thought and, in dialectic, by the negativity which ensures its dynamism. At every level negativity is what forces every figure of the spirit to turn into its opposite and to produce a new figure which has both suppressed and preserved the preceding one, according to the double meaning of Hegel's *Aufhebung*. Thus dialectic makes the tragic and the logical coincide in everything: something has to die for something greater to be born. In this sense misfortune is everywhere, but everywhere it is surpassed, to the degree that reconciliation always wins out over dissent. Thus Hegel can take up the problem of theodicy at the point at which Leibniz had left it for lack of other resources than the principle of sufficient reason.

Two texts are significant in this respect. The first is in Chapter 6 of the *Phänomenologie des Geistes* and concerns the dissolution of the moral view of the world; it is interesting that it occurs at the end of a long section entitled 'The spirit which is certain of itself' (*Der seiner selbst gewisse Geist*),[1] and before Chapter 7, 'Religion'. This text is entitled 'Evil and its forgiveness'. It shows the spirit divided within itself between the 'conviction' (*Überzeugung*) which inspires the great men of action and is incarnate in their passions ('without which nothing great is done in history'!) and the 'conscience that judges', represented by 'the fair soul'. Later it will be said that the soul has its own hands, but that it does not have hands. The conscience that judges denounces the violence of the man of conviction which results from the particularity, the contingency and the arbitrary nature of his genius. But it also has to confess its own finitude, the particularity disguised

---

[1] G. W. F. Hegel, *Phänomenologie des Geistes*, ed. Johannes Hoffmeister, Hamburg: Felix Meiner, ch. 6 1952, pp. 423ff.

in its claim to universality, and finally the hypocrisy of a defence of the moral ideal that takes refuge in the word alone. The conscience that judges discovers in this unilateralism, in this hardness of heart, an evil equal to that of the active conscience. Anticipating Nietzsche's *Genealogy of Morals,* Hegel perceives the evil contained in the very accusation from which the moral vision of evil stems. What then does 'forgiveness' consist of? It consists of the parallel withdrawal of the two elements of the spirit, in the mutual recognition of their particularity and in their reconciliation. This reconciliation is none other than 'the spirit (finally) certain of itself'. As with St Paul, justification is born of the destruction of the judgement of condemnation. But unlike Paul's view, the spirit is indiscriminately human and divine, at least at this stage of the dialectic. The last words of the chapter are: 'The Yes of the reconciliation in which the two selves withdraw from a being there opposed to each other, is the being there of the self extended to duality, the self, which in that respect remains equal to itself and which in its complete alienation and its complete opposition is certainty itself; it is God manifesting himself in the midst of those who know themselves as pure knowledge.'

The question then is whether this dialectic,

with logical resources which Leibniz did not have at his disposal, does not reconstitute an optimism which derives from the same boldness, but with a rational hubris that is perhaps greater still. What fate is reserved for the suffering of victims in a vision of the world in which pantragism is constantly recovered in panlogism?

The second text gives a more direct answer to this question by radically dissociating reconciliation, which we have just been discussing, from any consolation which might be directed to human beings as victims. This is the well-known section of the introduction to the *Philosophie der Geschichte* devoted to the 'ruse of reason', which perhaps itself constitutes the last ruse of theodicy. The fact that this theme appears in the framework of a philosophy of history already warns us that the fate of individuals is entirely subject to the destiny of the spirit of a people (*Volksgeist*) and to that of the spirit of the world (*Weltgeist*). It is even more precisely in the modern state, still in the making, that the ultimate end (*Endzweck*) of the spirit, namely the whole realization (*Verwirklichung*) of freedom, can be discerned. The ruse of reason consists in the fact that the spirit of the world makes use of passions which inspire the great men who make history and without their knowledge deploys a second intention, disguised in the prime intention of selfish ends that their passions make them pursue. These are the unintentional effects of the individual action which serve the plans of the *Weltgeist* by the contribution of this action to the nearer ends pursued outside each 'spirit of the people' and incarnate in the corresponding state.

The irony of the Hegelian philosophy of history lies in the fact that, supposing it makes meaningful sense of the great movements of history – a question which we shall not be discussing here – it does so very precisely to the degree that the question of happiness and misfortune is abolished. It is said that history 'is not the place of happiness'. If the great men of history are denied happiness by the history which they set in motion, what about the anonymous victims? For us, who read Hegel after the nameless catastrophes and suffering of the century, the dissociation between consolation and reconciliation brought about by the philosophy of history has become a great source of perplexity: the more the system prospers, the more the victims are marginalized. The success of the system brings about its failure. Suffering, by the voice of lamentation, is what excludes itself from the system.

Must we then give up thinking about evil?

Theodicy reached a first climax with Leibniz's principle of the better and a second with Hegel's dialectic. Isn't there another use of dialectic apart from totalizing dialectic?

We shall put this question to Christian theology, or more precisely to a theology which is said to have broken with the confusion of the human and the divine under the ambiguous title of the spirit (*Geist*), and which is said also to have broken with the mixture of religious discourse and philosophical discourse in onto-theology, in short, which is said to have given up the very project of theodicy. The example I have chosen is that of Karl Barth, who seems to me to have replied to Hegel, just as Paul Tillich, in another study, proves to have replied to Schelling.

5. The stage of 'broken' dialectic

At the beginning of the famous section of his *Church Dogmatics* entitled 'God and Nothingness',[2] Barth says that only a 'broken' theology, i.e. a theology which has renounced systematic total-ization, can engage in the formidable task of

---

[2] Karl Barth, *Church Dogmatics* III/3, Edinburgh: T&T Clark 1951, section 50, pp. 289–318.

thinking about evil. The problem will be to know whether he remains faithful to this initial assertion to the end.

A theology is broken which recognizes that evil is a reality that cannot be reconciled with the goodness of God and the goodness of creation. Barth reserves the term *das Nichtige* (nothingness) for this reality, to distinguish it radically from the negative side of human experience, which is taken into account only by Leibniz and Hegel. It is necessary to think of a nothingness hostile to God, a nothingness not only of deficiency and privation but of corruption and destruction. In this way one does justice to Kant's intuition not only of the inscrutable character of moral evil, understood as radical evil, but also of the protest of human suffering which refuses to allow itself to be included in the cycle of moral evil by way of retribution, and even to allow itself to be enrolled under the banner of providence, another name for the goodness of creation. That being the starting-point, how can one think beyond the classical theodicies? By thinking differently. And how does one think differently? By looking for the doctrinal nexus in christology. Here we recognize Barth's intransigence: Christ has conquered nothingness by annihilating himself on the cross. Going back from Christ to God, it has to be said that in Jesus Christ God has encountered nothingness and fought it, and that we thus 'know' nothingness. A note of hope is included here: since the controversy with nothingness is God's own affair, our fights against evil make us co-belligerents. Moreover, if we believe that in Christ God has conquered evil, we must also believe that evil can no longer annihilate us: it is no longer permissible to speak of evil as if it still had power, as if the victory were only in the future. That is why the thought that is made heavy in attesting to the reality of evil should make itself light and even joyful in bearing witness that evil has already been over-come. All that is still lacking is the full manifesta-tion of its elimination. (We should note in passing that Barth gives a place to the idea of permission from early dogmatics only to denote this distance between the victory already won and manifest victory: God 'allows' us not yet to see his kingdom and still to be threatened by nothingness.) In fact the enemy has already become a servant − 'a strange servant indeed', and one who will remain so.[3]

I shall break off my exposition of Barth's

---

[3] Ibid., p. 368.

doctrine of evil here, but hope that I have shown in what sense this dialectic, though broken, merits the name of dialectic.

In fact, Barth takes the risk of saying more — some would say too much. What more does he say about the relationship of God to nothingness which is not contained in the confession that in Christ, God has encountered evil and conquered it? That nothingness also relates to God, but in quite a different sense from the good creation, namely that for God to elect, in the sense of the biblical election, is to reject something which, because it has been rejected, exists in the mode of nothingness. This side of the rejection is in some way God's 'left hand'. 'Nothingness is that which God does not will. It lives only by the fact that it is that which God does not will.'[4] In other words, evil exists only as the object of God's anger. Thus God's sovereignty is whole, although the reign over nothing cannot be co-ordinated with the whole reign of goodness over the good creation. The former constitutes God's *opus alienum* and is distinct from his *opus proprium*, all grace. One phrase sums up this strange movement of thought: 'As God is Lord of the left hand as

---

[4] Ibid., p. 352.

well, He is the basis and Lord of nothingness itself.'[5]

This co-ordination without conciliation between God's right and left hands is a strange thought. We can ask whether at the last moment Barth did not want to respond to the dilemma that theodicy set in motion: if, in fact, the goodness of God shows itself in his having fought against evil from the beginning of creation, as is suggested by the reference to the original chaos in the Genesis narrative, isn't God's power sacrificed to his goodness? Conversely, if God is Lord 'also with his left hand', isn't his goodness limited by his anger, by his rejection, and should that be identified with a not-willing?

If we followed this line of interpretation, it would have to be said that Barth has emerged from theodicy and its logic of conciliation. In place of a broken dialectic we would have only a feeble compromise. There is another possible interpretation, namely that if Barth has accepted the dilemma caused by theodicy, he has rejected the logic of non-contradiction and systematic totalization that has dominated all the solutions of theodicy. In that case it is necessary to read all his propositions in

[5] Ibid., p. 351.

accordance with the Kierkegaardian logic of paradox and to eliminate every shadow of conciliation from his enigmatic formulas.

But we can put a more radical question: hasn't Barth gone beyond the limits which he imposed upon himself with a rigorously christological discourse? And in this way hasn't he reopened the way to the speculations of the Renaissance thinkers, taken up – with great power – by Schelling? Paul Tillich was not afraid to do what Barth both encourages and rejects. But in that case, how will thought guard itself against the excesses of intoxication which Kant denounces with the term *Schwärmerei*, which means both enthusiasm and mystical folly? Isn't it wise to recognize the aporia in which thought about evil finds itself, a characteristic conquered by the very effort to think more and otherwise?

III. Thinking, acting, feeling

In conclusion, I want to emphasize that the problem of evil is not just a speculative problem: it calls for a convergence between thought, action (in the moral and political sense) and a spiritual transformation of one's feelings.

Evil: A Challenge to Philosophy and Theology

1. Thinking

At the level of thought at which we are sometimes kept once we have left the stage of myth,
the problem of evil deserves to be called a
challenge, but in a sense which has never ceased
to become richer. A challenge is, in turn, a
setback for syntheses which are still premature
and a provocation to think more and in another
way. From the old theory of retribution to Hegel
and Barth, the labour of thought has never ceased
to enrich itself, prompted by the question 'Why?'
contained in the lament of the victims; however,
we have seen the failure of onto-theologies in
every age. Nevertheless, this failure has never
been an invitation to a capitulation pure and
simple, but rather to a refinement of speculative
logic. The triumphant dialectic of Hegel and the
broken dialectic of Barth are instructive in this
respect: the enigma is an initial difficulty, close to
the cry of lament; the aporia is a terminal
difficulty produced by the very effort of thought.
This work is not done away with by the aporia
but included in it.

It is to this aporia that action and spirituality are
called to give, not a solution, but a *response* aimed
at making the aporia productive; in other words,

at continuing the work of thought in the key of
acting and feeling.

2. Acting

For action, evil is above all what should not be,
but must be fought. In this sense action reverses
the orientation of our attention. Gripped by myth,
speculative thought is drawn back to origins. It
asks whence evil comes. The response – not the
solution – of action is the question of what is to be
done against evil. Attention is thus turned towards
the future by the idea of a task to be accomplished,
which matches the question of an origin to
discover.

It should not be thought that in putting the
emphasis on the practical struggle *against* evil we
again lose sight of suffering. Quite the contrary. As
we have seen, every evil committed by someone is
evil endured by another. To do evil is to make
someone else suffer. Violence never ceases to
restore the unity between moral evil and suffering.
Hence every action, whether ethical or political,
which diminishes the quantity of violence ex-
ercised by some against others diminishes the level
of suffering in the world. If we subtract the
suffering inflicted by some human beings on

others we shall see what suffering remains in the world; to tell the truth, we do not know this because violence impregnates suffering to such a degree.

This practical response has an effect at a speculative level: before accusing God or speculating on a demonic origin of evil in God himself, we should act against evil ethically and politically.

It will be objected that the practical response is not enough: first of all, as I said at the beginning, the suffering inflicted by human beings is distributed in an arbitrary and indiscriminate way, so that for countless numbers it is felt to be undeserved; the idea remains that there are innocent victims, as is illustrated in a cruel way by the scapegoat mechanism described by René Girard. Moreover, there is a source of suffering outside the unjust action of some human beings towards others; natural catastrophes (we should not forget the dispute sparked off by the Lisbon earthquake), illnesses and epidemics (think of the demographic disasters brought about by the plague, cholera, and even now by leprosy, not to mention cancer), ageing and death. The question then becomes not 'Why?' but 'Why me?' The practical answer is no longer enough.

3. Feeling

The emotional response that I want to add to the practical response relates to the transformations by which the feelings that nourish lamentation and complaint can undergo the effects of wisdom enriched by philosophical and theological meditation. As a model of these transformations I shall take the work of mourning as Freud describes it in a famous essay entitled 'Mourning and Melancholia'. He describes mourning as a loosening, one by one, of all the bonds which make us feel the loss of a beloved object as a loss of ourselves. This detachment, which Freud calls the work of mourning, makes us free for new emotional investments.

I would like to consider wisdom, with its extensions in philosophy and theology, as a spiritual aid to the work of mourning, aimed at a qualitative change in lament and complaint. The journey that I shall describe does not claim to be a model one. It represents one of the possible ways along which thought, action and feeling can go side by side.

The first way of making the intellectual aporia productive is to integrate the *ignorance* that it engenders into the work of mourning. 'No, God did not want that', must be said to the tendency of the survivors to feel guilty at the loss of their beloved object, even more so to the tendency of victims to accuse themselves and to join in the cruel game of the expiatory victim. Far less did God want to punish me. Here the failure of the theory of retribution at a speculative level must be integrated into the work of mourning as a deliverance from the accusation which in some way exposes suffering as undeserved. (In this respect the little book by the rabbi Harold S. Kushner, *When Bad Things Happen to Good People*,[6] is of great pastoral importance. To say 'I don't know why', 'Things happen like that', 'There has to be chance in the world', is the zero point of the spiritualization of complaint, made quite simply to itself.

A second stage of the spiritualization of lament is to allow oneself outbursts of complaint directed at God. The whole of Elie Wiesel's work takes this course. To the degree that the covenant relationship is a mutual one in which God and human beings must engage, it invites us to take this way to the point of articulating a 'theology of protest'.[7]

---

[6] Harold S. Kushner, *When Bad Things Happen to Good People*, New York: Schocken Books, 1981.

What it protests against is the idea of divine 'permission' which serves as an expedient in so many theodicies and which Barth himself tried to rethink when he made a distinction between the victory over evil already won and the full manifestation of this victory. Here the accusation against 'God' is the impatience of hope. It has its origin in the cry of the psalmist, 'How long, O Lord?'

A third stage of the spiritualization of lament informed by the aporia of speculation is the discovery that the reasons for believing in God have nothing in common with the need to explain the origin of suffering. Suffering is a scandal only for those who see God as the source of all that is good in creation, including indignation at evil, the courage to bear it, and sympathy for its victims; then we believe in God despite evil (I know the confession of faith of one Christian denomination, every article of which, following a trinitarian plan, begins with the word 'despite'). To believe in God despite is one of the ways of integrating the speculative aporia into the work of mourning.

Beyond this threshold, some wise men go in

---

[7] Like that of John K. Roth in *Encountering Evil*, Atlanta, GA: John Knox Press, 1981.

solitude along the way that leads to a complete renunciation of the complaint itself. Some come to see an educative and purgative value in suffering. But it immediately has to be said that this meaning cannot be taught: it can only be discovered or rediscovered; and it can be a legitimate pastoral concern to prevent the meaning assumed by victims from leading them to self-accusation or self-destruction. Others, who have progressed even further along this road of the renunciation of complaint, find an unparalleled consolation in the idea that God himself suffers and that the covenant, over and above its conflictual aspects, culminates in participation in the submission of the Christ of griefs. The theology of the cross – i.e. the theology according to which God himself died in Christ – signifies a corresponding transmutation of the lament. The horizon towards which this wisdom is directed seems to me to be a renunciation of the very desires, the wound of which engenders the complaint. This is a renunciation first of the desire to be rewarded for one's virtues, a renunciation of the desire to be spared suffering, a renunciation of the infantile element of the desire for immortality which would make the acceptance of one's own death an aspect of this part of the negative, from which Karl Barth carefully distinguished the aggressive negative, *das Nichtige*. Such a wisdom is perhaps sketched out at the end of the book of Job, when it is said that Job comes to love God gratuitously, thus making Satan lose his original bet. To love God gratuitously is completely to get out of the cycle of retribution to which the lament still remains captive, in so far as victims complain about the injustice of their lot.

Perhaps in the Judaeo-Christian West this horizon of wisdom meets up with Buddhist wisdom at a point that only a prolonged dialogue between Judaeo-Christianity and Buddhism could identify.

I do not want to separate these solitary experiences of wisdom from the ethical and political struggle against evil that can bring together all men and women of good will. In relation to this struggle, these experiences, as actions of non-violent resistance, are anticipations in the form of parables of a human condition in which, once violence has been suppressed, the enigma of true suffering, of irreducible suffering, will be laid bare.